OFF TOPIC

OFF TOPIC

POEMS BY

GRANT QUACKENBUSH

PINYON PUBLISHING

Montrose, Colorado

Cover Art "Grant Quackenbush" by Bradford J. Salamon

16" x 20"; Oil on Canvas; 2021; Private Collection

First Edition: October 2021

Pinyon Publishing

23847 V66 Trail, Montrose, CO 81403

www.pinyon-publishing.com

Library of Congress Control Number: 2021935255

ISBN: 978-1-936671-75-5

For Jeff Bezos

CONTENTS

III ALPHABET CITY

Open your arms like a fresh pack of cards
And shuffle the deck.
Now open your heart.
Now open your art.
Now get down on your knees in the street
And eat.

—Frederick Seidel

I

HOUSEPLANT

I water my ficus with milk. It grows
a mouth, sharp teeth. It yells at me.
"Asshole!" it shouts. "Put some Miracle-

Gro in here! Put me in a bigger pot!"
I do, and give it more milk. I feed it
meatloaf, bacon, porterhouse steak. Its roots

branch out the bottom and break
into legs, two twigs into muscular arms.
It sprouts a monstrous cock, hikes

its pot up like a soiled diaper. Smokes bud,
walks around. Does finger push-ups
on the ground. It opens my wallet,

removes a twenty. Dons my leather jacket.
When I rush to stop it, it shoves me.
"Kick his ass!" my wife says to the ficus.

She laughs, spreads her legs. Says c'mere
with her middle finger. The ficus grins. It enters
the bedroom. It plants in her its seed.

SOMETHING ELSIE

I once fell in love with an alien
named Elsie. Her real name

contained neither sounds nor signs
but was a sort of frequency which,

if you closed your eyes and focused
on your body, you could feel

graze the peach fuzz in your inner
ear. It worked best underwater.

Her complexion had a creamy
chartreuse hue to it like split

pea soup cut with powdered milk.
But since she lived in a human

host like a coffin, people thought
she was just anemic, not Martian.

She was something else, that Elsie.
An insatiable sex drive on top

of an incessant need to skydive.
She said she felt closer to home

up there, craved the touch of air.
She fancied herself a flying saucer.

She was a natural, she turned
professional. She set a world record.

But when the league discovered
she was green and didn't breathe,

she was banned from the sport
and deported to the moon.

81 & OVER

*"In my strip club
the girls crawl on stage
wearing overalls
and turtlenecks
then slowly pull on
gloves, ski masks
and hiking boots."*
—Denise Duhamel

At Herb's strip club
the girls are grannies
with diabetes.
They get wheeled out
onto a carpeted stage
by come-hither
caregivers who change
their diapers.
"Take it off!" the old
men in the crowd
shout in coarse voices
scratched by age.
They reach
into beige khakis, toss
handfuls of butterscotch
candies like gold
coins into a fountain
of youth. They drink
warm milk. Today
one of the boys
died from sudden cardiac
arrest, electrified

by his eyes. No one
seemed to notice
the team of paramedics
carting off the carcass
like a football
player in a stretcher
as the wonderful
Lethal Ethel
went around pinching
cheeks, swinging
her pendulous breasts
like a clock.

BLOCKHEAD

Be patient, poet. Verse
        cannot be forced.
                One can't just write

the word *Harley*, hop on,
        and coast down the virgin
                road of the page

anymore than one can
        draw a chalk door
                on a brick wall and pass

through it. Poems
        aren't cartoons. Nor are
                they voodoo. Shouting

Poetry! Poetry! Poetry!
        while whirling in front
                of a mirror won't help you.

Threatening the Muse
        with a sharpened
                pencil won't work either.

Best not to write tonight,
        find something less
                difficult to do. Make dinner,

love. Set a saucer of
        ink blue milk out. Let
                the poems come to you.

THE AVALANCHE

I spoke, and was spat on.
Spoke louder and was struck.
So I sat at a desk and wrote
in silence, determined
to someday make a difference.
I wrote and I wrote and I wrote.
I slept as a requirement.
When I had to eat, I ate.
When I had to bathe, I didn't.
I grew a beard, befriended a bird.
The seasons came and went.
It was the idea to wait
till the politics passed, release
the words all at once.
Finally, I did: I let them go.
An avalanche I hoped
would change the status quo.
But either no one cared because
no one heard, or no one heard
because no one cared.

AMERICAN DREAM

I like to pretend I'm a billionaire.
It takes the edge off being broke.
When I wake up in my shoebox room
which I share with a family of rats
(I hear them at night
playing Scrabble in the walls)
I say: I *choose* to live this way. I *like* rats.
When I go to work and the boss
tells me to move faster or I'm fired
I think: I could buy this shitty company
and sell it to *China* if I wanted.
Lah di dah dee, trah lah lah.
Sam Walton, founder of Wal-Mart,
drove a 1979 Ford pickup.
Henry Ford lived modestly in Michigan.
Look Ma! I'm Henry Ford
living modestly in Brooklyn!
I'm wiping my ass with wads of cash!
I'm the richest schmuck in America!
And no one knows it but me.

THE UPPER EAST SIDE

If you've ever visited New York City
you've probably been to the Met.
It's this gigantic ark of a museum
on the Upper East Side next to Central Park.
Six blocks up is the Guggenheim,
another famous museum. But I've never been *there*.
It's twenty-five bucks! Because that's the thing:
the Met's free. Or nearly. You pay what you want
if you live in the city.
(Each time I've gone I've only paid a penny.
I'm always confused by people who pay more.
I'll see them handing over ten-, twenty-, even hundred-dollar bills.
I'm like, Dude, you realize you don't have to do that, right?
But the Met depends on people
embarrassed to be perceived as *not* having money
so I guess it balances out.)
When I first moved to New York in 2017
I actually lived on the Upper East Side—on 72nd Street
by the train station with that never-ending escalator in it.
I say *actually* because
it's one of the most expensive neighborhoods to live in
and I was so broke I ate Trix
with a fork to save milk.
K, not really. But I *was* pretty broke. Before moving
I was working as a dishwasher in San Diego
and had managed to save up
just over two thousand bucks.
That meant I could afford a place
that was around seven hundred a month—
enough for first and last
plus money for beer until I found a job.

So I typed my price range into Craigslist and the next day
moved from the hostel in Bushwick I was staying at
to the place on the UES.
It was August but there was no A/C.
The sole window looked out onto a brick wall
painted in pigeon shit.
The bed it came furnished with
was a three-inch layer of orange foam.
The one bonus was the location.
Maybe *you* don't like ritzy shit
but I do because I've never had it.
Walking down the avenues there
with bellhops standing outside gilded hotels
and ladies in hats walking toy poodles
and business owners hosing off sidewalks
which the poodles had pissed on
despite signs that say CURB YOUR DOG
was like walking through Disneyland to me.
It was what I thought of when I thought of New York.
Brooklyn, Queens? Pshh.
Give me taxis and corking fees and hydrothermal manholes.
Give me suits and suites and selfies in front of the 9/11 Memorial.
Give me digital propaganda in Times Fucking Square.
Give me the Upper East Side!
Whenever I wasn't hungover
I'd get up before the sun crested the buildings
and walk the four blocks over to Central Park.
I'd get a triple espresso at Le Pain Quotidien
and sit down on a bench in front of a fake pond and read.
I'd imagine Salinger sitting there seventy years earlier
observing the great-great-great-great-great-great-great

grandparents of the ducks I was now observing.
And in the evening, if I wasn't working or getting sloppy at a bar,
to avoid going back to my hovel
I'd take a penny and go to the Met.
It's funny because I'm not even a fan of most art.
I just liked being there, surrounded by it.
When I moved to Williamsburg, then,
Land of the Hipsters,
it wasn't too long before I began to miss the UES.
But I never went back because my job was in Williamsburg
and there were plenty of bars to get drunk at there already.
Also because it was getting close to winter
and I'd heard the subway in winter
was an incubator for influenza.
If I could avoid it I did.
Then it was spring. Cherry trees
started blooming, parkas started shedding,
the East River started sparkling, sort of.
I thought how full of life Central Park must be
and remembered my old morning routine.
So on a Saturday when I wasn't working
I decided to make a day of it.
I'd go to the zoo, sit down
on the bench I used to sit down on,
walk on the dirt track around the reservoir,
buy a soft pretzel with salt and mustard on a corner
then go to the Met for a couple hours.
And maybe after I'd grab an IPA at a bar
and strike up a conversation with a beautiful woman.
I'd tell her my name was Chad Steele
and that I was a venture capitalist in town on business.

With my itinerary set
I took the L to Union Square
then transferred to the 4
which runs like a catheter up the big dick of Manhattan.
Right after it got going though
a shirtless, barefoot homeless dude shuffled in.
Having been in the city a while now
I'd seen my fair share of crazy bastards.
Not all of them homeless either.
I went out for a drink with this chick I met at Whole Foods
who said she was a gender non-binary vegan cat-loving socialist.
She talked about shutting down the patriarchy
as if it were a slaughterhouse
and her disgust with the disparity
between the rich and poor.
"You live in SoHo," I said. "You workout at Equinox."
"Your point?" she said.
But then there's the *homeless* crazy bastards,
their homelessness not the reason they're crazy
but their craziness often the reason they're homeless.
So anyway this dude walks in
smearing human shit across the floor
like a janitor doing his job in reverse.
He'd pinched a loaf in the space between the cars
and I guess had stepped in it getting up.
He hardly seemed to care.
He just kept walking, dragging his shitty foot
behind him like a zombie.
We all sat there and looked at each other
and didn't look at each other,
praying he wouldn't stop in front of us

14

and ask for change or a Seventh Generation baby wipe.
Of course when the train stopped at Grand Central
everyone rushed to leave, stepping over
the line of feces and out the doors
as other passengers filed in.
If you think I thought this was hilarious, I didn't.
But what was I supposed to do,
give the crackhead the penny in my pocket
so he could go contemplate a Picasso?
Virtue signal like that "woke" Equinox chick
but not really do anything?
No thanks. Instead I got on the next train
and went to Central Park Zoo
where I took an iPhone video
of seals doing tricks for fish.

LESSON

I was sitting on a bench eating Cheez-Its
when a homeless man came up to me.
I was a kid. Probably twelve.
I'd been skateboarding in a parking lot at the beach
and was taking a break.
"Spare change?" he rasped.
I'd seen him around there before. He was incredibly dirty
but moved too slow to be scary.
I said sure and reached in my pocket.
"You can put it in here," he said and held
a stretched-out condom in front of my face.
It had semen at the bottom.
"Jesus fuck," I said, grabbing my board
and standing up. "Get the fuck away from me
you crazy psycho."
That's when I learned
something very important.

ROOT CANAL

I have bad teeth.
I'm healthy otherwise but my teeth are horrible—
something to do with "soft" enamel.
So when during German
my bottom right canine started playing
Jimi Hendrix's *Star Spangled Banner*
I knew I had to go to Mexico
which, if you're fortunate enough not to know,
is where insuranceless Americans go for dental work.
Growing up in San Diego I'd go all the time.
You just drive to San Ysidro and walk across the border.
You don't even need an appointment.
The difficulty with *this* situation
wasn't just that this tooth hurt more than any other had ever
but that I was in college in Northern California.
Since I had less than two weeks left in the quarter
I decided to try to stick it out.
I applied gum-numbing Orajel, slept with my jaw on an ice pack
and, whenever the pain reached a climax
took a shot of Smirnoff, but like a craving for sex
the pain always returned.
It's crazy how a cavity can consume your life,
I thought on the red-eye home
having ditched finals for relief
and thought of the kid from Utah on my hall
who earlier in the quarter took LSD
and threw himself out his fifth story dorm window.

SELF-PORTRAIT AS
UNKNOWN PAINTER

Tonight, I dip
my instrument in oil
hoping to create
something someone
might interpret,
some somber
portrait of the artist
they'd turn over
in their mind
like an unsigned
love letter.

LETTER

I've been learning how to crawl.
Using my left hand instead of my right
to shave, throw Frisbees, draw. I look
through binoculars at nothing in particular, I light
candles to watch them melt. I cook.
When my ladyfriend asks me what time it is
I build a sundial out of rocks
and give her an approximation.
As a result, I'm single.
As a result, I know how to build one hell of a sundial.
I read maps, I take naps. I'm picking up the banjo. I press
my ear to the earth and just listen, listen.
I traded my Volkswagen in for a Schwinn. I quit my job
in order to stare out a window. I wrote this
with a pen.

2BGMACS

A man drives
      the blue truck
           of his body

down the tear-wet
      road of his heart,
           drunk. He cannot see

the others
      he endangers, hear
           their honks or shouts.

He drives. Days
      later, distracted
           by the weather, the bright

sun and what it
      could mean, he rear-
           ends the one

in front of him: a little
      red Corvette.
           They signal, turn,

meet in a McDonald's
      parking lot.
           The man falls

out of his body, offers
        the crumpled
                flower of a dollar. Asks

the lady driver
        if he can buy her
                a burger. He can.

DOING NOTHING

My favorite thing to do is nothing,
which is different from not doing anything.
Some people can't do nothing. They get antsy.
But me, I could do nothing
the rest of my life and be happy. If I win the lottery
I'm doing nothing with the money. I swear.
I'll buy a house in the South
and sit on the porch and stare, preferably
in a rocking chair. I'll drink
nothing but Coke and smoke only steak.
I'll play the fiddle and whistle.
If I need something I can't borrow or grow,
I'll start up my beat-up pickup (no one will know
I'm a millionaire) and drive with my Labrador
to the appropriate store.
I'll say hello to the owner, stop for soup
at a diner, then drive back home
into the quotidian sun, my dog riding shotgun.
And it will be like that.

AUTOSTEREOGRAM

We were supposed to be reading.
This was at school in the third grade
in the early nineties, when an hour
a day was still required and cursive
was taught alongside mathematics
and geography, weeks spent memorizing
the fifty states and the foreign capitals
we mispronounced, unknowingly
preparing our puckered lips
for the test of a kiss, in French:
BOIse, Des MOInes, Baton ROUge …
the rounded vowels like sour candies
in our mouths, like the lemon Warheads
we dared each other to suck on
until the sweetness came, or until
the five-minute bell rang. We spit out the candies
along with the cooties: recess, as we knew it,
was over. We sat inside reading, the click
of a stand fan oscillating back
and forth, cooling our ruddy skin.
Brandon slid a fuzzy picture over
the polychromatic pages of *Huckleberry
Finn*, whispering that if I looked
long enough, pressing my nose up against it
then slowly moving it away, like this,
a 3-D image would appear, in this case
a rhinoceros. Other times a palace,
a plane, a floating human brain.
It was called an autostereogram
and it became a sort of game,
a competition to see who could see

it first, decipher the message unconsciously
by staring, meditating on the art
of sin, letting our monkish minds
imagine. Half the time we saw boobs,
or wanted to. Randy said Ricky saw
dicks and everybody laughed. Except Ricky.
Ricky stopped playing, telling us to
grow up, homos, and pretty soon we all did,
more or less. Brandon became a manager
at a Jack in the Box downtown,
Ricky a professional chauffeur.
No one knew what happened to Randy
aside that he moved to Oregon
and a rich kid named Preston, as his name
might suggest, became a curator
at the Getty. I guess he lives in Pasadena
making big bucks, probably
spending all his dough collecting Pollocks.
I can see him now, stroking his chin
with his arms crossed, trying to distill
a meaning from what appears
to be absolutely nothing.
"It's pubic hair," his director
friend with a fetish for
cuckoldry concludes, just kidding
but not really: you see
whatever you want to see, whatever
you're bound to see
doing what it is you're doing
out there. When Manson was a kid
he saw murder in the sky, blood

leaking through the woolen sheets
of the clouds like acid rain—
through the coat of his neighbor's
Bichon Frise Yappy
he admitted to the cops to torturing,
holding a butter knife, he said,
up against its lamblike
throat and sawing, ripping off the head
as from a stuffed animal: dead.
But it doesn't have to be so extreme.
Brandon saw a burger and Ricky saw a car.
Preston saw a quarter and Jackson,
little Jackson from Wyoming
who used to like to ride ponies,
saw a bar. Woke up years later
in a pool of his own vomit like paint,
got an idea. Monkey see, monkey do.
And what did I see? What am I
going to do?
Today I went and sat
on the edge of a sandstone bluff
overlooking the blue lined pattern
toward the horizon. I put a hand to my eyes
to cut the midday glare and saw,
somewhat to my surprise, an island
off the coast of the mainland. I've come here
for years and had never seen it before.
So I looked again, and saw a boat.
So I looked again, and saw a whale.
So I looked again, and saw the sea, a surface
so bright you could write on it.

II

GROUP INTERVIEW

It was 2008, at the height
of the recession. I had dropped
out of college after consuming
a crop of magic mushrooms
and was now foraging for work
to fix my being broke, a fact
exacerbated by a nasty addiction
to coke. The problem was
there were too many people
to compete with. Desperate
Joes and Janes who'd been let
go from shops and chains
that had considered their positions
disposable income. Surplus.
A plus side to the unemployed
mass of applicants was that
the few places that *could* recruit
the occasional dupe or two
often did so through group
interviews, where all were equal
until proven unequal and nearly
anyone who wanted could go,
from former CEOs to hobos.
They were like AA meetings
but with less chance of recovery.
Speaking of drinking, Starbucks
was hiring. Which was ironic
since I'd been cutting my blow
with instant coffee to conserve it.
Side effects included buckshot
energy stalked by suicidal

thoughts and anxiety attacks
but I kept on using because
it wasn't an option to not
when like a pre-dawn train
the day of the interview came
and I showed up looking like
a spokesman for the living dead.
I was high. Ionosphere high.
Had my eyeballs fallen out
they would have shot into orbit
around my Ferris wheel head.
Instead my nose started to bleed
and the questions veered toward
me. I blamed the dry weather
even though it had poured
the week prior, a portentous
bank of sky having blown
in from above the rough ocean.
It was as if a supersonic jet
or giant Greek trident had ripped
a hole in the stretch denim
of the space-time continuum
that sucked all the moisture
from the unripe fruit of the future
then spit out rain like buckets of
coins from a slot machine, only
no one got rich. Just wet.
But soon the heat returned with
the sun like an NBA trophy
and increased the temperature
like the volume on a speaker

blaring the rock 'n' roll music
of light: dynamite bright, and hot.
So there I was, sitting in a cell
of a room like a sauna, dripping
drugged blood like sangria.
I excused the zombie that was
my jacked body to the john
where I wiped the warm
gore like a puréed rose
from my nose then sniffed
a venti-sized line of smack
with a buck. When I got back
the interview was almost over.
I sat. Everyone was going
around in a rectangular circle
stating where they would travel
if they could travel for free.
Three people said Hawaii, one
Russia in a Russian accent,
some dude in a suit the moon.
Shit, I thought. How's anybody
supposed to top that? I could
hear the anxiety arriving.
Yet I had to wonder whether
he actually meant it or just
said it to strut a rehearsed
outside-the-box wit because
to make like an astronaut
and leave this oxygenated planet
in a shut shuttle you cannot leave
because if you did you'd become

a snowflake drifting across
the perennial winter of space
would induce in my cerebrum
a hemorrhage of panic I'd pop
open the exit like a sealed
bag of chips to stop, to feel
for a suspended moment a sense
of expansion and of my place
in the cosmic entropic order before
drowning in a sea of stars
which reminds me of the time
I went on Supreme Scream
at Knott's Berry Farm at night
except I didn't go on if "went on"
means *rode* because I jumped
off before the metal leviathan
began levitating, stricken
by a rush of irrational adrenaline,
a feeling I'd get stuck
up there forever like that poor
fucker who got stuck in an elevator
for two days or maybe three
or four or eleven or a billion
if no one had ever pressed
the up/down button again.
Cover a rat with Tupperware
and it'll start thrashing against
the dome, suddenly aware
that it's *in* something—caught,
trapped. Unable to evacuate.
And I suppose a rocket ship

is one way of escaping
this warm terrarium of a world
just as suicide and psilocybin are
though it's possible you may
find yourself more cornered
than before, sent to some warped
black hole of a dimension
in which there is no door
you can punch in a code and push
open, parachute back down
into the downy safety of sanity
from the kaleidoscopic carnival
of your skull. But I wasn't about
to tell the interviewer that.
The interviewer with her green
apron and caffeinated grin
and pen poised above a clipboard
who was waiting like a customer
for my percolating answer.

OVERDOSE

His build was too slight
for the amount of heroin
he shot. His heart

slowed. Blood
became mud,
mud tar. He felt

a window shatter
in a bright
room inside him. Glass

flew like fanged
bats from his throat.
Someone spoke. He wasn't

breathing. He wasn't
doing anything
but staring at the ceiling.

SHOOTING PORN

I shoot porn
      into the open
            wounds of my eyes.

My face brightens,
      my pulse quickens.
            My dick stiffens

like a defensive
      porcupine. I shoot
            more, more. A dark

sea of dopamine
      floods my brain.
            My pupils swell

like blots of ink.
      I pant, I grunt.
            I might as well

oink. I can hear
      the love blood
            starting to boil.

A puff of steam
      escapes my manhole.
            It smells like bleach.

It burns my hand.
      It lures the thirsty
            leech of my mind.

I shoot. The blunt
     needle of my phone
          contracts a virus

that sparks a chain
     reaction of pop-ups.
          The screen cracks,

my bliss peaks.
     My head erupts
          with salacious thoughts.

TWO ACTS

"I and the public know
What all the schoolchildren learn,
Those to whom evil is done
Do evil in return."
     —W. H. Auden

1

We were in junior high
 riding the bus going
to school, boisterous
 as usual: screaming out
windows, jumping
 over seats, shooting spit
wads at girls we liked.
 Being kids. The driver,
Mr. Warner, told us
 to put a lid on it. We did.
He turned the radio
 up. A soft voice spoke.
Some sort of attack,
 thousands likely dead.
That's all I understood.

2

September. Fall weather.
 Still summer, yet not.
Lag between dreams,
 intermission between acts.

A time to go outside
    before you must go back
inside. A time to chat,
    smoke, note the rocking
red oaks, the scattered
    leaves like shattered
glass. Listen. The wailing
    wind, the crashing ocean.
The rubble of glowing
    rose petals everywhere.
And, standing there: us.

POSTWAR

Joey Poiriez, a skateboarder
October 3, 1986 – April 20, 2014

And if alien archaeologists
should discover our bones in the future,
there having been some terrible
but inevitable event—the broken

boards of our femurs, the compressed
accordions of our spines; hips and teeth
chipped or missing, ankles shot, both
knees blown out; staples in our skulls—

they would postulate a war our planet
had suffered, guess the weapons we'd used
to cause such pain, devastation.

O, Joey. We're bones already, skeletons
skating the earth. You only went first,
too fast. Let me find you again.

SITTING ON A BENCH AT
MOONLIGHT BEACH

October in Encinitas, and the day
comes to a close. The sky turns
pink, then lavender. Bonfires
burst like solar flares on the shore.
In the distance: faint light
from a boat, the long sigh of a train.
And then this blooming
wound lodged in my chest, this blue
rose I call my heart. I can feel it
dropping cold petals into my gut.
I can feel it raining inside me.
O, world! It hurts so bad
it makes me want to leave you, to know
this music will end. So loud, the song,
and then it's over—embers
spiraling up toward the stars.

RED TIDE

If I should ever decide
to do it, I'd do it
swiftly with a shot
on a beach at night,
on a sloped shore
leading down to the water
reflecting light.
No one would hear it,
not even me.
But at midnight,
when the moon
would cause the ocean
to swell, to suck into
its chest a deep
breath of waves and
exhale them like hands
over my head, washing
away the red,
it would grab me by
the ankles, the tide,
and gently pull me in
and under.

KÜNSTLERROMAN

I took a bite
of a red book
like an apple. Words

spilled from my
mouth like seeds.
I took another

bite. Another.
The pages churned
like white waves

within me. They formed
strange sounds,
loud verbs, foreign

nouns. They filled me
with energy.
I spoke for years

in what I thought
was English.
No one understood

me but me.
I tried using
signs, my hands,

a megaphone.
People furrowed
their brows, walked

away. I shouted,
cursed, sang
into a recorder.

But all I heard
when I played it back
was wind in trees.

NOT THE GREAT POET

One's life is purpose-driven,
and that purpose is to become
a poet. A great poet. A poet
who will transcend the art.
As one ages, however,
and is confronted by reality,
one's view of poetry
changes. *Too niche. No return
on investment. Dumb.*
The passion kept hidden
like a secret power as a youth
seems now unimportant.
Fucking seems important.
Owning a Tesla seems important.
But poetry, poetry
does not seem important.
Yet from time to time, perhaps
out of reason, perhaps drunken
emotion, one tells oneself
that it *is* important, the sublime,
then sits down and writes
what is (regrettably) not.

THIS MORNING,

after putting on a sweatshirt
I left on the floor last night, I felt something
feathery tickle the back of my neck
so wiped it with my hand and saw, crawling
on my hand, a not-very-big black spider.
"EeeeeyaAHHH!!!" I screamed,
flapping my wrist and flinging the spider
to the carpet. "*Motherfuckshit,*"
I spluttered. (I had the heebie-jeebies.)
Keeping it in my sight
I grabbed an anthology of *The Best American Poetry*
and dropped it on top of it, pressing down
like a paramedic on a chest.
"Sayonara," I said. But when I lifted
the book up, the spider wasn't dead.
It looked like a booger, tinged with blood.
Its broken legs gave little kicks.
Would you believe me if I said I glimpsed
myself in that moment, a crippled old man
suffering before death?
I placed the book back over it
and pressed down, harder.

ROAD KILL

You pull over on the side of a road
and you look at it: what is it? Or, maybe
you should ask what it was before you hit it: nothing ever,
by the looks of it. The more you look at it
the less sense it starts to make, like
a Rorschach test and the lifeless words
used to describe it: black, white, flat ...

Leave it alone. It's done. And by "done" I mean
finished before it began. There's no use
in trying to save it, breathe it back
into a shape. The most you can do is
bless it and move on, tell others
a long time ago you thought you saw one, whatever it was
or could have been.

SATURDAY

He woke up in a bathtub, not so much hungover as he was still drunk. He felt woozy. His mouth was dry. His tongue was a swollen cat's, his nose a bat cave of shit. That night he had been offered cocaine. He had accepted. He had also taken a cold shower with all his clothes on, including shoes, after yelling "I'm gonna die! I'm gonna die! Somebody help me I'm gonna die!" That's when he woke. Or, not so much woke as regained consciousness. He was soaked. He was shivering. He picked a sharp, blood-encrusted booger like a stalactite from his right nostril with his left thumb and flicked it at the drain. It transferred to his flicking finger. He flicked it again and it stuck to the shower wall. He left it. Outside the windowless bathroom he could hear the murmurs of morning voices. He hated those voices. He felt repulsed by those voices. He dreaded opening the door and walking out past the people who spoke them, saying hello, good morning, how are you. He thought he heard his name. Suddenly he remembered he had to be at work at seven a.m. He had to help open the doughnut shop he'd been hired at the week before. He took his flip phone out of his pocket. Broken. Milk blue light flooded in through the space beneath the door. He would be fired. That much was certain. And then what? The same thing over again? He thought about his rent and how it was due. About his mom who he paid his rent. "A hundred dollars," she'd said. "Just so you can start contributing." But he couldn't even manage that. He thought briefly of the future and of his place in it. Of the things he would have to do as an adult to stay alive. It frightened him. He stood, farted, undressed with difficulty. Wrung out his socks, jeans, Joy Division T-shirt, then put them back on with even greater difficulty. He went to the door and pressed his ear against it. Waited. Waited some more. When he could no longer hear any voices, he turned the knob and stepped out into the day.

III
ALPHABET CITY

6/8/18

Anthony Bourdain committed—
despite enjoying fame

given his international job/
kickass life meeting nations

of people (Quebeckers, Romans …)—
suicide. Tony, unlikely victim:

why X yourself?
                    Zounds.

X MARKS THE G-SPOT

"I gave a horse a blowjob."
—Grant Quackenbush

Abecedarians annoy the shit out of me. To go from A to Z
because that's what the form demands is, in a word, crazy.
Can't poets find anything better to do than write complex
doggerel no one gives a damn about but them? I mean how
egotistical do you have to be? Answer: Very with a capital V.
Forgive me if I seem insensitive. It's just that frivolous froufrou
gets on my nerves. Speaking of poetry that makes me petulant,
have you read Grant Quackenbush? Don't. He's atrocious.
I produce sweeter verse from my ass. But seriously, I'd rather
jam a fork in my eye than be forced to read that hack GQ.
Kanye West—now *there's* a poet. Well, if you consider rap
lyrics poetry, which you'd have to be a total moron not to.
Music, after all, is akin to poetry. One could say it's its twin.
(Note that *lyric* comes from *lyre* and *rhyme* from *rhythm*.)
Others agree. Bob Dylan, you may recall, won the Nobel
Prize in Literature in 2016. But I digress. Back to that quack
Quackenbush. I heard from a source he gave a horse a BJ.
Raunchy? Yes. Really? Eh. Honesty isn't my modus operandi.
Some of you might be wondering why I'm talking so much
trash. To reiterate: I despise Grant's writing. It makes me gag.
Urinary tract infections are more appealing than the decaf
vanilla piss he passes off as poetry. He should call up Kanye
West, solicit his advice. Write a poem in his honor called
"X Marks the G-Spot." I don't know. Something eccentric
"Ye" would approve of. As long as it's not one of those dumb,
zany double abecedarians of his. They're worse than diarrhea.

DELIRIUM TREMENS, *PART 1*

"My kingdom for a nuclear gin fizz."
—Barbara Hamby

"ABS! ABS! ABS!" the TV screamed. "Call 1-800-EAZY-ABZ
by January 1st to claim your FREE consultation today!"
Calling would've been tough, though. I'd lost my iPhone X
drinking at a bar the night prior where I sniffed some POW-
erful "nutritional powder" this tattooed vegan Bev
from Beverly Hills told me was like super good for you.
Granted, I didn't believe her. But she was asphalt-
hot and I was stone-cold drunk so I gave her fifty bucks
in exchange for a line and a high I don't remember,
just regret. When I woke I was missing my vintage Shaq
kicks not to mention my iPhone (X!!!), faux Rolex and backup
loot which I'd put in my tube socks. I looked like a hobo
minus the bindle: barefoot, bearded, sleeping on a bench in
Newport Beach. Ugh. I'm not sure if it was the rum
or a lack of water or (more likely) that so-called nutritional
powder but I hadn't been so hungover since I took
Quaaludes and tequila shots at a Mexican discotheque in TJ.
Right then I decided I was done. Finished. *Vincit qui
se vincit.* He conquers who conquers himself. A rough
translation by which I simply mean I had sworn off drinking.
Until that evening, that is, when I quaffed half a bottle of
vodka to calm my head. This was back in Oceanside
where I was watching an exercise infomercial in bed.
Xmas was over and I was in worse shape than ever. A horrific
year for my liver. I thought about taking a taxicab to rehab,
zonked out instead. But not before taking a long drag of vodka.

DELIRIUM TREMENS, *PART 2*

Around noon, after catching a few hallucinatory Zzz
below the glow-in-the-dark star stickers forming the imaginary
constellation of my ceiling, I fixed myself some Trix
downstairs. But all I could do was stare into the rainbow
eye of the bowl like a lobotomized nut staring at a busted TV.
Forget cereal. What I needed was a warm café au
gin, a shot of alcoholic medicine to soothe my ginger root
hands like a friend, keep them from trembling like palm trees
in wind. I felt queasy, as if I were reading in a vortex or
jalopy. The bowl with the spoon in it became a capital Q.
Knowing what was coming, I hunched over and abruptly threw up
lime-green gunk that smelled like a skunk taco con mayo:
malo. So there I was, hungover again, an injured birdman
nursing my pain by regurgitating on the linoleum,
owl-style. Well, bozo, there goes that infomercial
promo, I thought, glancing up at the microwave clock:
quarter to one. New Year's Day. I figured I'd make a PB & J
rye bread sandwich since it was lunch (though a martini
sounded better) but the only bread I had was brick-hard French.
(True fact: the word for "bread" in French is *pain*. Just saying.)
Unemployed and behind on rent, I couldn't help but wonder if
very many millionaires struggle this much with life,
what with wads of dough and all. I might as well have had
X's for eyes my body was so exhausted, not to mention toxic.
Yet how I hungered to change! To sparkle! To burst from the Rob
Zombie double I was into something beautiful, once larva.

2007

At the time I was living in the lively town of Santa Cruz
between San Francisco and the more boring town of Monterey,
California. (I specify CA because there's a Monterrey, MX—
double *r*, though.) People in those parts are slightly askew,
especially in Santa Cruz. I knew this dude who lived in an RV
for free in the woods illegally and read nothing but Thoreau,
Ginsberg and survival guides. He was a self-described pacifist/
hippie, though last I heard he'd joined the Marine Corps.
(Ironically he used to jack liquor from what he called "Traitor
Joe's" because they supposedly supported the war in Iraq.)
Kooky vagrants, however, aren't the only ones who shop-
lift booze in Santa Cruz: underage undergrads do too.
My freshman roommate, a potbellied pothead who lived on
nachos and Coors, had a fake ID that said he was a midget from
Olowalu, Hawaii. Off topic: did you know the Hawaiian al-
phabet has just *thirteen* letters!? Anyway, my perpetually drunk
quadruple-chinned roomie, who looked kind of like Ignatius J.
Reilly from the book *A Confederacy of Dunce*s, tried to buy kiwi
strawberry vodka for a party but got caught like a prize fish,
the ID having flopped. Long story short he resorted to stealing.
Unfortunately I was making pretty shitty decisions myself,
virtually all of them involving drugs. Although I never did like
weed very much. I preferred pills and coke. Once I even snorted
Xanax while on ecstasy. But enough about college at UCSC.
You're probably sick of listening to the red bird of my mouth blab,
zipping around my head. So as they say in Hawaii: aloha!

EMAIL TO A YOUNG POET, RE: ADVICE?

All right, listen up. First what you want to do is blend Ritz,
bananas and orange juice together until you get a creamy
consistency. Add ghost pepper hot sauce, Ex-Lax,
Diet Pepsi, gunpowder, a glass of gasoline and a dozen raw
eggs for protein. Blend again, and enjoy. I call it a Molotov
fruit smoothie because, like a Molotov cocktail or fu-
gu, it's liable to kill you. Either way it'll turn your butt-
hole into a flamethrower the next day when you pass gas.
If that sounds gross or dangerous, consider all the other
junk people (myself included) ingest: rubbery burgers from DQ,
Kentucky Fried Chicken, All You Can Eat pancakes at IHOP …
Look. The point I'm trying to make with all this mumbo jumbo
Molotov talk is that you have to learn to cope with pain.
Noxious amounts of it. And not temporarily, but ad infinitum.
Otherwise you risk becoming not a poet but a mental
patient who chops off his ear and drowns himself in drink.
Quit writing if you can't handle a little gasoline and OJ.
Rejection will hurt more. Trust me. It'll feel like a samurai
sword sodomizing your ego without lube. Van Gogh
took his own life it hurt him so bad. Preferred pushing
up daisies to living broke and unknown. RIP. So punch yourself
violently in the nuts. Give a sumo wrestler a piggyback ride.
Watch a beauty pageant while guzzling the aforementioned
XXX smoothie. Get used to pain to make rejection less tragic.
Young poet: good luck. I'd ramble on but I have a date with a sub-
zero walk-in freezer. Naked. I'm trying to contract pneumonia.

NYC ABC

April is when the fun begins—in the Big Apple at least. Jazz
bands come out in full swing to sing spring. NyQuil is replaced by
cocktails on rooftops (ever had a Manhattan?). Even the *T. rex*
dinosaur that resides on the Upper West Side (which you can view
every day at the Museum of Natural History) seems less frozen as V
formations fly above it like planes exporting people with the flu.
Goodbye, flu! Goodbye, dirty snow! Goodbye, cracked-out
hobos who hibernate throughout the winter on the trains!
Is that offensive? I hope so. Few things in life give me greater
joy than offending the easily offended. It's delicious. So are BBQ
kettle chips, but that's beside the point. Hey, is that Johnny Depp?
Living in New York City you see celebrities all the time. And O-
MG: the women! Nowhere on earth are there as many stun-
ning, braless, promiscuous twentysomethings than here in Gotham.
Once, for instance, I was reading *Tropic of Cancer* in Central
Park when a brunette with big tits walked by. I dropped the book,
quickly asked her out and later that night she drank my splooj.
Romantic, right? That's the beauty of dating here vs., say, Abu Dhabi:
sex is granted almost instantly. It's awesome! If you approach
ten women at random, have game and are decently good-looking,
usually five of them (including the married ones) will be DTF.
Visit, reader, and you'll want to stay. That's what happened to me
way back in 2017 when I hopped on a plane from the relaxed
Xanadu of San Diego to the hustle-and-bustle metropolis of NYC.
Yes, it can sometimes suck ass. But so can living at home in a suburb
ziplocked inside a town with no nightlife, pussy or 99-cent pizza.

A BRIEF HISTORY OF MY LIFE: ZERO TO THIRTY

"There was I: a stinking adult."
—John Ashbery

Although I tell people I'm from San Diego, I was actually born in Mesa, AZ but moved when I was two. That was in 1990, before Internet pornography, cell phones and social media gangbanged our lives, to say nothing of Netflix. Don't mind me. I'm just being my usual curmudgeonly self, a trait that grew exponentially in adulthood. Specifically the first couple years, when an SUV full of reality hit me. (For some reason I'm picturing a souped-up Subaru.) Generally speaking childhood was a blast. All I did was skate. But yeah, post-high school was a shitshow. I went to UC Santa Cruz, did a bunch of drugs (including one called sassafras), then dropped out and enrolled in a two-year junior college where I took a remedial math class and learned to solve for q—knowledge I didn't care for, so dropped out again. Talk about a nincompoop. Luckily I've never had trouble finding a job when I needed one. I've had so many I can't remember them all. I've worked at a gas station, a strip club, In-N-Out Burger for a month (I got "terminated" for not showing enthusiasm on top of eating fries while serving customers), plus dozens of random retail places that didn't require any skill. Throughout this time I was getting drunk quite often. Like everyday. I drank this mix of shit called jungle juice (aka JJ) round-the-clock. Then fate introduced me to a book by Charles Bukowski. Suddenly a sunlit valley opened up before me. It was like a giant light switch turned on. I was filled with hope, excitement. A feeling I'd found my calling, unprofitable as it was: poetry. Needless to say my early poems were knockoff versions of Bukowski's. Imitation crab meat. I even bought a dusty IBM typewriter because that's what *he* used to use but the apparently popular *s*, *e* and *x* keys were broken. To fast-forward (I'm spent), I met *une jeune fille du Québec*, yielded to her advice to stop drinking and start eating, quit my judicial job zapping roaches and a decade later got an—ahem—incredibly lucrative MFA.

58

POLITICAL POEM

"A few cubicles away a mild, ineffectual, dreamy creature named Ampleforth, with very hairy ears and a surprising talent for juggling with rhymes and meters, was engaged in producing garbled versions—definitive texts, they were called—of poems which had become ideologically offensive."—George Orwell

A far-left progressive purple-haired feminist from Uz-
bekistan who was in my MFA program at Boston University
claimed all cops should die. She also worshipped Marx,
despised America and considered herself a militant SJW.
Evey, the naive damsel turned terrorist in the movie *V
for Vendetta*, wasn't even as extreme as this BU
girl who, by the way, said white people are inherently racist.
"Huh?" I said, and informed her that that was
itself racist. But she just accused me of "attacking" her.
Judge one another not according to skin color, nor IQ,
King said (I'm paraphrasing), but according to important crap
like character or whether you uphold freedom—a memo
most poets these days seem not to have gotten.
Not that there's anything wrong with writing a poem
once in a while. It's just that fanatical leftists and the political
poetry they produce has hijacked the art. And it's all junk.
Quash dissident opinions, says the new order. Label Donald J.
"Rump" and anyone flaunting a MAGA hat a Nazi.
Suppress free speech that expresses "hate speech."
To say the left has gone cuckoo would be a misleading
understatement. They're a cult that practices self-
victimization. Why? Because victims are untouchable,
which means if you criticize them they can call you a bigoted
xenophobe and get you fired. It's as easy as ABC.
Yay for love! Yay for inclusivity! Yay for this culturally drab
zeitgeist fueled by identity politics and a radical agenda!!!

—summer 2019

THE LAST POEM I'LL EVER WRITE

"MFA programs have turned poetry into an occupation, and a joke—have turned it into one or more subject in a university or private scam operation."
—Franz Wright

Arguably the worst decision I ever made was to go into the poetry biz.
Biz isn't the right word though since there's no money in poetry.
Clowns make more peddling balloons, and they don't shell out x
dollars per year to read books where *x* is over 50,000 at New
England University. 200K to put some bullshit BA on your CV!?!?
Fuck that. It's better to have no degree and work at a drive-thru.
Going off to college as a phone-addicted teenager to major in art
history or literature or cultural anthropology because it sounds
intelligent is stupid. Most likely you'll graduate with debt up to your
jugular just to be able to count in French: *un, deux, trois, quatre, cinq* ...
Kids, don't pay to study the humanities. They're a financial trap.
Learn a skill that's actually marketable, like mixology or auto-
motive repair, neither of which require an overpriced education.
Now, combine the absurd cost of tuition with the growing problem
of censorship on college campuses and it's no wonder normal
people (if you just got offended you're a politically correct cuck)
question the value of taking classes taught by wackos high on Mary J.
Remind me again what I was talking about? Oh yeah: my genius deci-
sion to become a poet. Not only is it impossible to generate cash—
that is, unless you're handed an award and land a gig at some big
university—but if you disagree with the elite your career will go *poof*.
Vanish. All this is to say this is the last poem I'll ever write.
Why invest time in something that will only lead to a dead end?
Xerox the above and distribute it, then, because no academic
yearbook of a press will ever publish it for fear of inciting a mob
zookeepers couldn't keep at bay. If asked who wrote it, say: No idea.

NOTES

In "The Upper East Side," the sentence "We all sat there and looked at each other and didn't look at each other" is from Bukowski's novel *Factotum*.

With the exception of "6/8/18," which consists of twenty-six words in alphabetical order, the poems in Alphabet City are all double abecedarians: the left side of each poem goes A through Z down the alphabet, and the right side goes backwards Z through A down it.

Off Topic is not intended to reflect the author's life or views. It is hyperbolic and fictional. As I write in "X Marks the G-Spot": "Honesty isn't my modus operandi."

ACKNOWLEDGMENTS

Clementine Unbound: "Doing Nothing," "Road Kill"

Cordite Poetry Review: "This Morning,"

Cultural Weekly: "Houseplant"

Forklift, Ohio: "2BGMACS," "Letter"

Muzzle: "Autostereogram"

Orange Coast Review: "81 & Over"

Rattle: "American Dream," "The Last Poem I'll Ever Write"

San Diego Poetry Annual: "Blockhead," "Email to a Young Poet, RE: Advice?," "Künstlerroman," "Overdose," "Postwar"

Tammy: "Group Interview"

Westwind: UCLA's Journal of the Arts: "Delirium Tremens"

ABOUT THE AUTHOR

Grant Quackenbush grew up skateboarding in San Diego. He received his MFA from Boston University and his BA from the University of California, Santa Cruz. This is his first book.

CPSIA information can be obtained
at www.ICGtesting.com
Printed in the USA
FSHW010417300621